Dreams Are My Social Life

Dreams Are My Social Life © 2023 by Rupert Wondolowski is licensed under CC BY-NC-SA 4.0

First published by Publishing Genius Press in 2023

ISBN 978-1-945028-51-9

Publishing Genius
PO Box 328
Westport, NY 12993

www.publishinggenius.com

Cover Art by Christine Sajecki
Back Cover: "Image of the 'Black Sun', from *Splendor Solis*, a German alchemical treatise, 1582" via *The Public Domain Review*, publicdomainreview.com

DREAMS ARE MY SOCIAL LIFE

RUPERT WONDOLOWSKI

G PUBLISHING GENIUS PRESS

CONTENTS

Dreams Are My Social Life
1

Rehearsal for Hysteria
2

The Winter Made Many Demands of Us
3

Tulum, 1989
5

Faulty Haunting
6

inside a tree
7

You Climbed Party Face
8

Snow, Tree Forts, and Alcohol
10

Like Most Things the Scrap Heap Has Changed
12

Summer Labor
13

On the Matter of the Pinched Baby
14

Brautigan
16

A Shoebox Versus a Church Versus a Swimming Pool
17

"The heart is a rage of afflictions."
21

Tears Are Time Travel
24

I Am Balding, He Is Balder, Hair Is for Girls
26

A Visionary Friend Is Gone, Long Live His Vision
27

I'm going to lie on my side in my cupboard and grow potato eyes
30

1963
32

Strawberry Xanax
33

spring makes me small
34

Pills
35

I'm Not Listening to the Beatles, You're Listening to the Beatles
37

Seeing Beckett in February with Megan
40

For Everly
44

a table made of grandma
45

In the Neighborhood
46

Some Late Night Thoughts of Mortality While Staring Glassy-Eyed at Karen Black
47

Once Upon a Flaneur's Magpie Dance
49

The Faces it Held
51

Consumer Pivot
53

They Made Cough Syrup Bitter So You Wouldn't Put it on Your Pancakes
55

Lines Composed Upon Waking in James' Apartment to a Long, Disheveled Form on the Couch, Its Head Lolling Over the Edge, Revealing a Glistening Wig of Curls that Had Me Reaching Inside My Doctor's Bag for My Scalpel
56

Where the Road Peters Out Beyond the Old Sawmill
57

Things to Do Around a Wild-Eyed Drunk
58

Dreams Are My Social Life

We were beyond restless.
We changed parking lots—
again.

Time is muscle torn
back in the mindwebs
of that musty bar.
Summoning holes of grief
to pour sweet granny caulk into.

A little owl seamstress
made a cottage from
the day's textile picnic,
but then that guy doing
Cherry Bombs fell through it.
Please don't let the light
be from a road cop's flash,
and don't step in the back room
with Mullet Mike.

Rehearsal for Hysteria

Pencil sentence for profound symptom. Sorrow folds common.
Tablecloth train, probably ungodly.

Barbed. Memories of bandages through window, aggro organic.
Pine resin will never leave you. Potatoes won't shut up.

The Winter Made Many Demands of Us

Coffins and storms
carried away
much that we loved.
The sky joined us in our heads,
an elegant rattling ensues
&
agony—
until the curtain between worlds splits
and scary shit comes out.

There is no safe place
outside the tree fort
or Peter Pan's rec room.
It's easier to take
with a nice chilly breeze
and a couple blankets on at night.

Who's sitting here waiting
for this cobweb,
selling carpeting
from bankrupt motels.

A jellyfish could
unlock
the secret of immortality

recently returned
from a tanning products
convention in Nashville.
Green effulgence
or rejected swain
it's the 13th inning
after midnight.

Right now I'd like to be
the reflection in a
mirror
of a lake outside a window
as a gnarly hand pops out
clutching

the bloodied white rag
of peace.

Tulum, 1989

The lean dogs with tight rough fur roam the beach at night. Red star Antares is so large and close you can hit it with a tequila slingshot.

He self-medicates asthma with cough syrup, breathing wet sandpaper as he hears the shout of the German sitting in the outhouse, a snake lowering from an overhead beam.

The beautiful little girl runs into their cabana, tells them to come to her house.

The family's room is warmly packed. The television shows images of San Francisco wracked by an earthquake. A young woman on the screen who looks like Bo Peep crouches in a doorway convulsed by a belly laugh.

Faulty Haunting

>Daily corridors feasting on mirrors
>where even the flat dull butter knife
>has early Kubrick resonance
>when Hal is working
>the counter tremblified.
>There's no escaping his
>breath of tin and rye toast.
>In his earwax-misted windbreaker
>there is a tiny pocket of anger—
>everything happens to fit in there.
>If you smoke enough night and
>release your teeth you will
>forever muff a jangle in Nevada
>soothed by eyebright
>banged by the gong of gone.

inside a tree

inside a tree's hollow
among the moist and
becoming
becoming
something else
at the foot of the
tree without shadow
sparrows take the breath
from a trapped
child
the convenience store
isn't all that far
its yolky light
a hovering womb
beets bounce liquid
fire on flagstone
is this the gnome's life?
will there be baths?
pale smoke in your satchel
clam skins on
your kneecaps

You Climbed Party Face

No, that moon
the one way over there
I clung like
a biker's leather
pants in August
to it one desperate
night and forty
gazing down
on
slacing tadpoles
in giant construction
mud pond
broken things
more numerous
than fires
at the old Duncan Place
start with hearts
end with plumbing
squandered maps
found on backs of
fleeing meth mother's
legs dragging child
to next fruitless caper
you can find your dead
in oil streaks on

highway puddles
or seated immobile
among spent ketchup squibs
in a scowling
Hip Hop Chicken
I've gotten
my shit together
since I lost weight
and can easily slip
through windows
to steal copper
out of basement walls

Snow, Tree Forts, and Alcohol

There were rock battles in the claymines.
Shingle tile fights in the tree forts.
Crabapple wars in the backyards.

The one kid with a ridiculous last name
that was a foodstuff that doubled as yet
another slang word for penis killed his
girlfriend while the rest of us were
sort of thinking about college.

The brother of the guy who put his
cousin's eye out with a whipped roof
shingle that had a couple rusty nails
in it, killed a friend in a bar fight.

The fellow up the street who
looked like a young
Michael Stipe or Gene Wilder—
big puffs of cottony hair swarming
his slender face—was involved in
high school theater one year ahead of me
held out until he was an adult to kill his wife
and leave her body out in some far-flung field
in order to be with the local barmaid.

The skinny blonde who got straight A's and liked to pick something out of his eyebrows and eat it all the time, reacted to the deaths in Bhopal by saying "Those people lived in tents. How dare they ask for so much cash for damages?"

And I keep thinking of my parents hounding me, saying "Why don't you go out and play football with those boys?"

Like Most Things the Scrap Heap Has Changed

Your wings are gone
Reinvent flight where that old school used to stand
Find someone with a lot of teeth
to deliver threats to that fucker holding all the balloons
Next door doomsday prepper parents
give birth to a sweet little kerosene lamp
who just wants to shine on the unfortunate

My sister was mistaken for French
while standing in the Louvre
If I stand long enough in night
will someone take me for the moon?

Summer Labor

The construction crew was more than happy to call it quits early, even though half the time most of them crept in late, hiding behind the rolling lunch cart. The universe conspired in their desire. That summer was filled with cool gray rain. The boss stuck a nailgun in a live socket, the current throwing him against a wall. Monday morning the crew that did the primary work, getting the outer walls up, had simply disappeared, their trailers gone, among rumors of gangster connections and tax fraud.

One bright day in the sunniest of sprawling backyards, the middle-aged customer walked right through a closed sliding glass door like a bankrupt magician. That night the crew went to a fat plaid couch party. Beige walls said more than the tight-lipped beer drinkers. The apprentice carpenter went out to his cousin's truck, feeling heavier than a thousand years. He let Lou Reed's "Rock n Roll Animal" on 8-track play endlessly and drank toward blackout.

On the Matter of the Pinched Baby

For Susana Harris

> I'm no longer so sure
> who pinched the baby.
> It wasn't a locked door mystery
> or anything. Just the presence of
> newborns creates a swirl of manic
> energy and rising anxiety and an
> edgy bliss, and at some point there
> were a bunch of the family in the
> living room and then not so many
> and then the dinner table was getting
> set and something good came on the
> radio and then the baby was crying
> and its upper arm and right cheek
> were red and puffy.
>
> But everyone turned out fine
> until it hit the point that some
> were not doing so fine and a few
> started falling apart and one or two
> died, but most of it seemed according
> to what felt like a proper schedule.
>
> And for years I always spoke

with great fondness for my
father's French Onion soup and
everyone always agreed
Then one day someone said "He never
made French Onion soup, he made
blank soup" and everyone agreed and
I can't even remember what soup they
were now saying he made because it
just seemed wrong and I
know I never ate it.

Strangely, what I do know
for certain, what I saw
with my child eyes and made
sure to confirm with my father
months before he died because
a friend suggested I had dreamt it,
was that long ago my father
and other dads of the Y Indian Guides—
suburban men all—
dressed in full drag, including
wigs, one night while camping
to disturb the cranky park ranger.

This memory sustains me.

Brautigan

When I gaze at the sky
When I sip my coffee
When I cross an idle street
I think of hippy moms

A Shoebox Versus a Church Versus a Swimming Pool

Shadows dump the
voices of frustrated
payphone calls into
the shoebox, along with
an unimpeded box car
moustache that once
rode above lips tossed
with indigestion.

The church is filled
with hushed marching and
a brocaded cushion
feels boundless yearning
for the swinging
incense canister.

A swimming pool can
be a baptismal, so
blue and rippling and topped
with shifting light
triangles, but it can
also be a fondue
pot of greasy bodies
doing things that

humans do in what
some may call their
mortal weakness.

For the disgruntled
onlookers things are
at a maddening crawl
as they yell for
blue suede shoes
reflected in Cadillac
chrome, Germanic angels
lifted from Deutsche
Gramophone covers
aloft in trees,
roaring stadiums or
at least wrinkle free collars.

There is a slow
closeup pan on
a heavily veined hand
lifting a photo of
Uncle Divshek from
the still crisp shoebox,
its corners not yet
blunted or kicked around.

Which indicates that
there might still be
hope, that someone has
bought new sneakers
or wingtips for
a fresh school year
or job interview.

After surviving the
Battle of Bastogne
Uncle Divshek refused
to fly unless the
pop band The Beatles
were also on
the plane, reasoning that
no god would take
them down while they
were so beloved.
Which is not saying much
for Buddy Holly or Patsy Cline.

In this photo
Uncle Divshek has his
arm around his
parish priest by

the side of the
neighborhood pool.
A few days after
it was taken,
two altar boys were
found floating dead
on the pool's surface
and Ringo Starr
was killed in a hunting
accident by the
Vice President of
the United States.

"The heart is a rage of afflictions."
—*Leonard Cohen*

>The air felt great today.
>I saw the unmistakable head
>of Mighty Joe Young floating
>inches above the calm water
>of Lake Roland.
>
>There was a fantastic electronic symphony
>of hatched bullfrogs.
>
>Not even Denver Boot talking
>grotesquely loud on his cellphone
>under the bridge about his toxic
>mortgage could ruin my day.
>
>After my dog rolled ecstatically
>in a vague heap of something nasty
>he came up with the perfectly cleaned
>skull of some long dead creature.
>I placed it in my jacket pocket
>and we set off towards
>Little Debbie's Equinox Party.

On the way there a man dressed
business casual sitting in a car
asked me where a woman could
buy pepper spray to protect herself.

Little Debbie's old friend Paperclip Eye
had filled the moat in front of her cottage
with trumpeter swans and REM sleep.
A group of proud boastful cossacks
sat in a circle around the beer keg.
When I asked them for a Clamato juice
they tried to cajole me into playing
the hot new video game "Grandmother Beat-
down."

Little Debbie's old college dorm mates
The Midday Terrors were playing an
overtone-rich power drone in the backyard
as people who were soon to be lovers
twirled among feathers, colored glass beads,
lace and church windows.

When Debbie told me the drummer's sister
had just died I handed her the skull
my dog unearthed.
"This is just like the skull I used to have
on my stick shift," Debbie squealed.
"It was lost and now it's found."

The linguist who lived in a
rain culvert on a woodlot
answered by plopping some
of God's flesh in his mouth.

Tears Are Time Travel

I didn't feel well.
Granny let me stay
home from school.
45 years passed.
Father died.
Like a champ.
Didn't even dip into
the painkillers the
hospice left in plenty.
The night before he went
I asked him how he was doing.
He said "Okay, I just have to beat this."
The day he died
bulldozers started tearing
at the woods behind our house.
A long feared and protested event
happening now like a staged
scene in a John Sayles movie.
Mother died.
Not so good.
Howls of the soul so
twisted and agonized that
a lifetime of horror movies,
Catholic school
and Flannery O'Connor

could not prepare me for.
I hunted mushrooms
in my backyard woods
wearing soggy Batman slippers
with my granny.
I'm still there.
I'm pretty much here.

I Am Balding, He Is Balder, Hair Is for Girls

For Neil Feather

He said it was good to hear my chuckle of the damned.
We decided we both had the mantra "lazy coward."
A recounting of the body down the slippery slope.
We both knew everyone else was doing much better.
But as a therapist might say, *define better*.
But first define therapist.
My old one dug feverishly in her ear.
A real Fudd going down the twisty hole
for a wascally wabbit scenario.
She arrived late to our first meeting and said
What does this tell you?

A Visionary Friend Is Gone, Long Live His Vision

For Chris Toll

Though not a licensed phrenologist, I would have to start with his head, his majestic hairless skull. "Ambient light from a Lenin Lightbulb," is how Bed Bath Blavatsky & Beyond put it.

He had thought it into a handsome planet of clearly defined paths, culverts and landing strips for minute travelers of all dimensions to set down on. His poems of quiet passion were the generator for untold powerful landing signals.

Often when out at night he would gently bow his head and rub a spot, saying "I've brought many visitors with me tonight."

There are those of us who sculptors should memorialize into busts and those of us who would be more suited to Jell-O molds. For the virulent, languishing in a potato sack as they bleed out in a donkey cart across the border as their captor bitches to a neighbor "*no se puede vender el gringo dañado,*" is the only proper final tribute to their cranium.

For my friend, Lost Astronauts Who Knew Too Much work in a sealed chamber in deep space with the DNA of Helen Keller, silky webs spun by spiders surrounding Poe's crypt, and the tears of broken hearted Catholic school girls to create the hands that will one day bring the dimensions of his dome into such glory that Rodin's bust of Balzac will shrink into a PEZ dispenser out of embarrassment.

About his small smooth arms, what can be said that has not already been stated by a multitude of paleontologists about those of the late lamented T-Rex? The surprising disproportionate strength of them could perhaps best be measured by the incident when he shared the dias with populist poet Billy Collins. My friend got up to read right after Collins finished his somewhat musty, frequently trotted out, "Mother's Day" poem. Shaking hands with Billy before taking his place behind the podium, the shake went a few moments beyond the norm and Collins' face contorted into a wide grimace before a small shard of bone pierced the skin of his forearm.

I will leave it up to YouTube viewers as to whether there was a trace of a smile on my friend's lips as Mr. Collins tried to muffle a shriek of agony.

It would take a book to enter into his heart and do it justice. Nancy Drew in fishnets would find Jesus in there playing lightning bolt toss with Dr. Strange. Drinks hoisted aloft to the downtrodden in a vast castle filled with toys, Bob Dylan passed out on a giant feather bed covered with absinthe bottles.

I woke up to my friend gone from my planet this morning and the goneness had gained immense weight. Struggling into my shirt my shoulders had an attitude—"Yeah right, go ahead, put a shirt on." Even my car windshield had tears on it on such a cruel sunny day. My friend you should hear this, this beautiful song that's playing. My friend you wrote such beautiful songs.

I'm going to lie on my side in my cupboard and grow potato eyes

Hang out your shingle & huddle
The stuff being said out there
would make a carnival barker blush
My poodle's going to grow a pair
& take out some trash

As fast as you can mutate
the world contorts in
painful spasm
& you're BETA
debased
not even groovy old
VHS tape in thrift store

Do you find yourself making
motorboat noises with your lips
Do you find your digits
among the weeping
diapers loaded Vegas dice
Are your footsteps tax compliant
Can your heart do the dog

Our table on the 18th green
had shrapnel popping in the gin
The one gunman stopped long enough
to grill and eat meat

I'm making a car wreck face
Mirror you know nothing
I was a little girl bike
A knotted old man seeking upright

If the spine of the exploded terrorist
plopping onto the cop car windshield
does not signal the
end of civilization
what mythology can
we now grow
to make room
for all our breath?

As my Amish friend says
"It wonders me."

1963

He speaks well through well-enforced glass. Keeps strict law among star-faced moles while I stay at home lit by a pair of crystal hurricane lamps. Enthralled by stereo, moon shots and color TV. Nat King Cole sweaters carry the sun down. A misery lands electric. John Kennedy dead.

Strawberry Xanax

Shuffling dance in a hot air balloon
squares in a crop circle
discussing Brubeck
Heimlich refuting reflux
and wishing for the
return of jive
or at least
a decent tea towel

The second time you're told
you'll drown in a river of blood
it loses some of the chill
it sends down your spine

The third or fourth time
it's another trash fire
in the backyard
and gets stuffed
you poor child you have
lice eggs in your hair
where you no longer reach
cut off at the knees

spring makes me small

I am not as cheerful
        as my shirt would indicate
    or as horrified
as my hair

in between the seething
        pause
    fur can be futile
and jackals make good dads

tumble me this yoga mat
        a sun rises from my
    ribcage into my throat
and there just isn't room for it

Pills

All night there was a hard rain
on the old tin roof.
The rain was pills.
A torrential downpour of pills.
Turn on the shower, pills.
Swirling down the graying drain,
gaudy colored Janet Leigh heads—
or pills.

With breakfast there is the kitchen TV
(the most modest in the house)
and it speaks of all the latest pills.
Why to take the pills—
What for to take the pills.
How you'll feel.
Under the milk truck
trumpeter swans
and fuzzy priapus
sweater are common.

Beaver Scouts scale a
cascading wall of pills.
An actor plays a doctor
dispensing pills.
In his office you are preceded

by a young salesperson
dressed like Vegas who
has dragged in a showcase of pills.
On the walls are pictures
of pills, pills descending
illustrated human networks.

On the street there is the one
who is off his pills.
Red-faced stalker.

Or the one swimming past
her gullet in too many pills.
Her chin has folded up
into her cheeks through
a beige flap of fear.
Each passing mouth
is one pill away
from the answer,
or a breakdown,
or a stunned liver.

I'm Not Listening to the Beatles, You're Listening to the Beatles

I grew up with two
older-brother musicians,
fell asleep to the needle stuck
 on John Mayall singing
"Standing by the deep blue sea"
even more times than
thinking the clothes on
the wall peg were
a murderer.

Immersed myself way too early
in the deep boggy sadness
of Leonard Cohen,
some days pulling the curtain
after school to cry to
"Songs of Love & Hate."
Middle brother did a killer bluegrass version
Of the Velvet Underground's "Heroin"
turning "Heroin, it's my wife, it's my life"
into an earthy country chorus.
He also would beat me up on occasion
if he caught me listening to WCAO
which actually mixed it up pretty good
for an AM station, it being the '60s, early '70s.

Sure it would play the maudlin bubblegum
of "Sugar Sugar," "Seasons in the Sun," and
"Alone Again, Naturally," but it
would also cut loose with Sly Stone
and James Brown, much to my shaving
father's morning chagrin.
"It's Dark in the morning."
Took me far too long to realize
he meant, the deejay,
that his name was Johnny Dark.

Either way, it was early poetry for me.

Neither brother would abide the Beatles
though the eldest did a mean Donovan
and Cat Stevens, when not reading
esoteric books of black magic and sorcery
once crashing my mother's bridge club
late at night, still asleep,
white boy fro a jumbled tower,
speaking in groggy
terror of a lucid dream he just tore himself
away from where he was doing battle
with an evil spirit.

He once wanted to be a priest
and when he saw *The Exorcist*
on opening night
his hands remained tightly
clawed for days.

When Middle Brother had overnight guests
I would sleep in the room on a cot
or in the ancient tiny bunk beds
with mummy pillows that would
make my neck and head creak
and stick like our sour grandfather's—
a man as welcoming as
a brown Ohio field in July.
I was up when he and a woozy
stoned and drunk pal came back
from seeing *Easy Rider* when it
opened and blew things up.
I heard "Captain America"
mentioned a lot and I was definitely
down with that, but could only guess
at the revolutionary feeling they had caught
and shiver at the talk of rednecks with guns.
The next night he glued my
fingers together with Super Glue.

Seeing Beckett in February with Megan

There was little air in the air
that day,
it being a February Sunday.
Dead leafless trees
a warehouse for crosses
were king, jutting gravemarkers in
the static cold dampness.
It was a day made for a hospital visit,
for putting on an old sweater
and finding a nest of unraveling.

Megan, who has raven black hair,
at that time could go a day without speech
except for the heavy metal amped
through her eyes.
She was wearing her sky dust
robin's egg
detective raincoat and
 Krapp's Last Tapes
was being performed
in the university's converted barn.

We swam through the gray day
to see John Astin, the original
Gomez of *The Addams Family*—
a show that informed my childhood
of anarchy and true love—as Krapp.
It was said to be his last performance
that he was leaving the university.
That information slid into the gray sack.
I wondered what would become of
the parallel library he had built here
to match the one he had in California.
Each of his book purchases so gleeful.
He would lift the Albee play and draw
out its name like Krapp elongating "sspppoooollll."

I spot an older poet friend who I
met as a customer in my bookshop.
Often Amanda and I watched
his old car struggle its way to our door
and we'd cheer it on.
His son at one point
played violin on the street corner
near where I bought coffee
& I looked forward to
his keening notes & wave,

his long thin hair a sun flag.
The old poet's ahead in line
With his entire family,
they're having a Beckett
Sunday outing, maybe to be
followed by a meal of silent
bananas in the nearby graveyard.
May the slippery skins
trip up hissing persistent phantoms,
ever at our heels.
I will be the hovering gooseberry
recently rolled off a pantseat oiled pew.
They were the only light of the moment
barn lights lowered for
Krapp's emergence.

I wave, they wave, we move our
mouths without words.

There is a communion of language
inside the barn, a hush
for an emissary of life's tender agony
to reflect on everything on this muckball—
all the light and dark and famine—
feast if you got it—

better than a kick in the crutch.
"Are you still up for daisies tonight,"
Megan asked
while under us all moved
and moved us gently
up and down, side to side.
Stop
and listen
to the bells.

For Everly

Late afternoon flecks on her arms as the
Canadian uke man jumps about like Jiminy Cricket,
giving his audience of six heartfelt atomic
razzle dazzle.   Her hand on mine, the sense of
everyone's gathered breath, the blast of coffee—
I've waited decades for this:
Drop the feeling into a river and watch it spread
                    in far reaching ripples.

a table made of grandma

swell fulsomely for the birds
a seething squelch of a liver hotel
you don't need to be Florida
to hang those meats in your raincoat

dad's got something in a sack
gliding eye to eye
with skunk cabbage
he never stops for highway food

it's only the smell of graves
cypress knees and dead stumps
hold me, smell my breath
tell me if I'm hallucinating

In the Neighborhood

The happiest I ever saw Rodney was the day he drank rubbing alcohol by mistake
    He came rushing across the street to tell me so.
    The second most happy was when he popped in and said "My doctor took me off all my heart medications"
    A few weeks later he was dead.

Some Late Night Thoughts of Mortality While Staring Glassy-Eyed at Karen Black

Look at you all chased by shin
high tribal fetish with razor sharp
spears! That little fucker wouldn't
give up! Or bug-eyed and winsome
courageously daffy, really
among a family of eccentrics.
The Ping Pong kept them human,
tables were everywhere in the '70s
and the silenced Poundian father
gave them gravity.

Dithering alone to Tammy Wynette
without realizing you're alone.
It really, truly, does often all
come down to trapped
in a truck stop restroom
either puking and pregnant
or puking and deserted
staring at what's left
in a smeared reflection
passing for a mirror.

If you only knew
what was coming—
the global crash
the toxic air
the hurricanes
and floods—
you would grab
a few of those handy
rolls in the john
and construct what
is known as a shirker's nest
and wait out a few nights.

If you think those hairs
on your chicken leg
were gross just wait
until Ronald Reagan
is upheld as a hero.

Once Upon a Flaneur's Magpie Dance

For Linda Franklin

> A rubber chicken lodged in a tree.
> High enough you don't remove
> you point and remark
> beating the snow off your boots
> outside the door the tree
> grows sentry by.
> Only to have the branch crack
> years later in a storm
> on a day surely your heart
> will burst from any more inky blackness.
> The sodden weathered chicken hitting
> the cracked ramped pavement.
> Its time and season bleached lips
> belching up two, three, maybe four gold coins—
> such are the visits from Linda.
> "I found this leaked caulk
> that looks like a snail.
> Here, I'll put it in your window
> for all to see. It'll be your North Star."
>
> Her eyes are periwinkle and winking
> always processing inner transmutation
> involving bubbles, think spaghetti and chopped

and screwed Chuck Jones cartoons.
"I found these old shoes on a gnome
out by the briar patch
and I thought why just change shoes
when I can change my feet?
Now I have no idea where
I'm walking and I love it."

Tiny toy clowns hidden on bookshelves.
Boxes of required paper scrap reading.
Harmonica lessons from Daddy Stovepipe.
Tales of rib joint Rufus Thomas
and standing by the childhood bed of Elvis.

"Take a picture of me by the 8-ball
in my scary mask and fisher hat."
"Take a picture of me by the 8-ball
in my floppy painted shoes."
"Take a picture of me by the 8-ball
with Dina, with Rocco, with Sailor Magee."
Take a picture oncemore
quoth the Linda
and maybe one and many more.
We are all taking in water, waving adrift
while Linda juggles on the shore.

The Faces it Held

Gathered friends traded
horror stories of college roommates—
my spoiled rich kid
sadly the worst.
Sending his mother up on arrival
me sleeping off my first
dorm party in August
drenched not so tight or
white whiteys
old banana peels
suckering to my young nates.
He bought outrageous items
without discussion and asked
me to pay for half.
I walked back from class
one night to find him
reading my girlfriend's letter
to me out loud to
four fellow hall creeps.

Meanwhile Megan had a literal rug
pulled out from under her.
Waking up as roommate
tugged it, saying
"Oh, didn't I tell you,

I'm moving in with Bitsy Grayscale."
By day she spoke of
dating the basketball star
purely for his fame.
By night she had one
beige wash cloth that
she repeatedly used to
scrape off the bold impasto-
applied pancake makeup slathered
like a basement Pollock.
Night after night the faces
were removed and gathered,
the cloth never washed.
When she finally left
Megan in peace she may
have taken the rug and
cost Megan that morning's
sleep, but the cloth
remained hanging,
stiff with the faces it held.

Consumer Pivot

Trust me, approaching hooded figure, I'm holding two bags worth of spending, it would not be worth arm swinging or darting blunt object to send me gravel sprawling.

I am an upright fleshbag of hobo stew. Cut me and the sins of my dank meals spill out. Forgive me mother. Forgive me Jesus. For what I've put up in here. So much of it after midnight in the maybe there's no tomorrow hours. Never a temple, but once it was a grassy playground. A high school friend almost wrecked her car because she was looking at my ass.

I just had a birthday. I'm thinking of death. More than as a morose white teenager listening to Simon & Garfunkel, staring out at December snow. Barely able to play another game of Stratego.

I'm nearly bald. These are not wispy wings that remain but unraveling yarn of befuddlement. The top and tip of my skull has a long dent which I never noticed until my shabby canopy collapsed. Sadly my mother is dead so I can't ask her. "You have failed at life and you ask about some crease on your big old head?" I show her my first book of poetry. She cries. I take the recording of my poetry on the radio and play it in her hospital boombox. She runs from the room.

Another, cruder crease to my head would probably impede my further efforts at attaining cash or friendship.

There is my famous friend Jason of the all encompassing moony eyes who was accosted in an alleyway by one more desperate than yourself. Gun out desperate. Jason's soothing tone and wise words reflecting his vast life experiences and weird psychic antena eventually had the would be assailant sobbing weeping and they hugged. The two of them eventually started a little candleshop in the boutique neighborhood of Hampden in Baltimore and were even approached by an insurance company to be their spokespeople.

But you are rushing at me, hooded figure, from the other side of the street, you are stage shouting something—"this is the down side of late stage capitalism"?

One day my clattering crouched mcsquatty by the lowest row of gifts led the Wockenfuss candy ladies, who thought the store was empty, to mistake me for a ghost. How much fun would it be to be a candy shop ghost? But not being one here beneath the dirt rug, beside the battered pavement.

They Made Cough Syrup Bitter So You Wouldn't Put it on Your Pancakes

It was a shining moment to explore
the deepest recesses of your stomach with
the gnawing teeth of anxiety.
To promote old pieces of clothing
to "Most Lucky" or "Most Comforting."
To watch slasher movie marathons
as homeopathic remedy.
Things fell from the sky.
Things that should not have been
in the sky went up there.
Clown shoes were found abandoned
as the escaped jokers climbed
the unguarded scaffolding of public acclaim.
Breath was watched.
Hands barked by washing and praying.
The rivers swollen with hat racks,
Mylar balloons and Silicon Valley startups.
Kerouac's Ant Orchestra plays on, but
with bent trombones and crenelated tubas.
There is nothing without the
proclamation of frogs at dusk.

Lines Composed Upon Waking in James' Apartment to a Long, Disheveled Form on the Couch, Its Head Lolling Over the Edge, Revealing a Glistening Wig of Curls that Had Me Reaching Inside My Doctor's Bag for My Scalpel

Shane and his cheeks are a big old karoake hashtag
He's all like, "I look like Kurt Vonnegut" and
I'm, "No, no, you crashed my lemonade stand
with your jet ski
You're a basketball hairdresser
Shampooing a wedding cake"

The trail was nutty with buttercups and cardinals
When do you sit with your chin
Down to your knees, Mr. Moritz?
Spill.

Any minute now Tom Cruise is going to
Walk in and fire everybody.

I toot your bubbling fantastic
vibrating in the beer spill neon
Your dance tells me
where the best flowers are.

Where the Road Peters Out Beyond the Old Sawmill

Lacking shoe
Gone disturbing
9 miles of Needmore

You know the vibes are right
When the balloons
Cling to the wall

Having cordial relationships
With wax figures
Drowsing in the oil flame light
Noses plopping in laps

Bic lighter and tank top
$2.95 Schlitz sixer

She sleeps like a
Washing machine spin cycle

Things to Do Around a Wild-Eyed Drunk

Climbing Snyder's Skeleton

Wrap up in a blanket and just read.
Practice writing Chinese characters with beer tabs.
Paint pictures of the police outside.
They are not there for you.
Repeat to yourself.
Put out salt for deer.
Stare at iron oven and wish you were better.
Hours off hunting twisty firewood, thinking
where morbid clowns could hide or
guy wearing his mother's face could pop up.

I made bargains with Ruth about which Grand
Canyon mornings
I'd rise for with the sun and which I'd sleep through.
Even wrote a schedule.
She ignored the schedule.
Sunsets are mercy for everyone.

Rolling blackouts.
The books the dog chewed.
The many books the dog didn't chew.
Old *Reader's Digests* left behind.
We'll soon be in the clouds.

Oily saws wrapped in musty weather.
Forest Service sleeping bags retain
the form of bare girls.
I can't name the peaks,
I tried to enjoy the climbing.
I ended the night in foggy socks,
a shallow pool of snowmelt.

Acknowledgments

Some of these poems appeared previously in the chapbook *Mattress in an Alley, Raft Upon the Sea,* published by Fell Swoop.

"Shoebox Versus A Church Versus a Swimming Pool" was published in *Everyday Genius* and then in the anthology *I Wagered Deep On The Run Of Six Rats To See Which Would Catch The First Fire*, edited by RW Spryszak.

"Lines Composed Upon Waking…," "Where The Road Peters Out Beyond the Old Sawmill," and "Things To Do Around a Wild-Eyed Drunk" were published in *The Nervous Breakdown*.

About Rupert Wondolowski

Rupert Wondolowski is also the author of *Mattress In an Alley, Raft Upon the Sea* (Fell Swoop), *The Origin of Paranoia as a Heated Mole Suit* (Publishing Genius) and *The Whispering of Ice Cubes* (Shattered Wig Press). He performs in The Mole Suit Choir and Wondofeather and lives in the fabled land of Baltimore.

A FEW OTHER BOOKS IN STOCK AT
PUBLISHINGGENIUS.COM

Fudge by Andrew Weatherhead [POETRY]

Modern Massacres by Timothy Willis Sanders [SHORT STORIES]

Subtexts by Dan Brady [POETRY]

Madness & Memory by Paula Bomer [ESSAYS]

Night Moves by Stephanie Barber [YOUTUBE COMMENTS]

Valparaiso, Round the Horn by Madeline Ffitch [SHORT STORIES]

Lilith, but Dark by Nichole Perkins [POETRY]

Steep in the Boil by Megan McShea [POETRY]

Eat Knucklehead by Craig Griffin [RECIPE LETTER NOVEL]

Michael Kimball Writes Your Lifes Story on a Postcard by Michael Kimball [POSTCARD LIFE STORIES]

Pee on Water by Rachel B. Glaser [SHORT STORIES]

Nobody Dancing by Cheryl Quimba [POETRY]

Yr Skull a Cathedral by Param Anand Singh [POETRY]

I Don't Know I Said by Matthew Savoca [NOVEL]

Irksome Particulars by Matt Cook [APHORISMS]

Sprezzatura by Mike Young [POETRY]

www.ingramcontent.com/pod-product-compliance
Lightning Source LLC
Chambersburg PA
CBHW030351100526
44592CB00010B/917